Cambridge English Readers

Level 3

Series editor: Philip Prowse

D1743746

Two Lives

Helen Naylor

CAMBRIDGE
UNIVERSITY PRESS

CAMBRIDGE UNIVERSITY PRESS
Cambridge, New York, Melbourne, Madrid, Cape Town, Singapore, São Paulo

Cambridge University Press
The Edinburgh Building, Cambridge CB2 2RU, UK

www.cambridge.org
Information on this title: www.cambridge.org/9780521795043

First published 2001
8th printing 2006

Printed in the United Kingdom at the University Press, Cambridge

A catalogue record for this publication is available from the British Library

ISBN-13 978-0-521-79504-3 paperback
ISBN-10 0-521-79504-4 paperback

ISBN-13 978-0-521-68648-8 paperback plus audio CD pack
ISBN-10 0-521-68648-2 paperback plus audio CD pack

Illustration by Jason Walker

Contents

Characters

Part 1
Huw Thomas: a sixteen-year-old coal miner.
Gareth Thomas: Huw's brother.
David Thomas: Huw's father.
Megan Jenkins: a sixteen-year-old schoolgirl.
Harry Jenkins: Megan's father.
Part 2
Beth Jones: Megan's daughter.
Philip Jones: Beth's husband.
Paul: Megan's fiancé.
Mike: Huw's son.
Rebecca: Mike's wife.

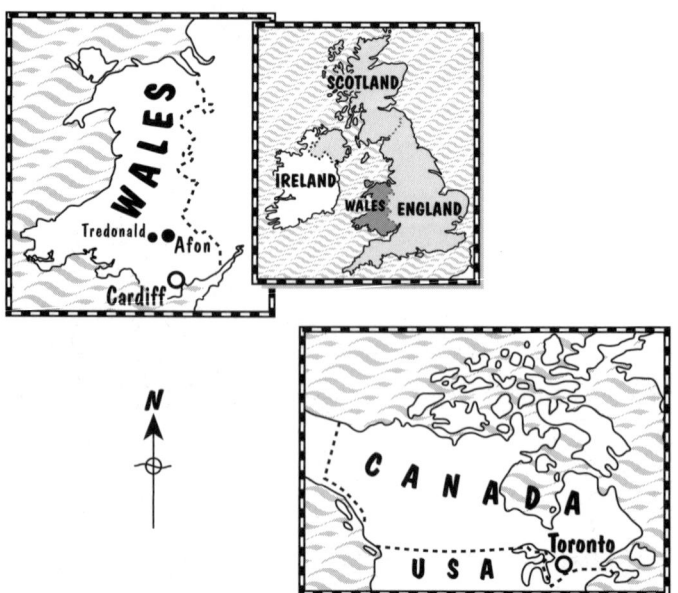

A coal mine

Prologue

My dear Huw

It was so good to get your letter. And thank you for the photos. It was good to see that even after all this time you haven't changed much. Wish I could say the same about myself!

Your letter produced a lot of different feelings in me – I was very happy to see how well you've done in life – I always said you could be a great artist! But I felt sad, too, that I hadn't been part of it. We had so many plans when we were younger, didn't we? But we mustn't think about the past. There's so much we have to talk about now. Beth and I are both very pleased that you've decided to come to Tredonald – let me know when you arrive in England.

With all best wishes
Megan

PS Here's a photo of Beth and me which was taken in the sitting room above the shop. Remember?

Part 1   Young love

Chapter 1   *Two young lives*

March 1945

'Megan, make me a cup of tea, will you?' shouted Harry Jenkins from the front of his small shop. 'And then come in here and talk to me.'

'Here you are, Dad,' said Megan, giving him a big cup of hot tea and trying to smile. Every day it was the same. As soon as Megan got home from school, her father asked for his tea and then he wanted to know everything about her day – what she had done at school, if the teachers were pleased with her work, who she walked home with. She was sixteen years old and she was fed up with it all. Why did he have to be so interested in her?

'So, Megan, how was school today?'

'OK,' said Megan.

'Did the teacher tell you about last week's exam, then?'

'Yes.'

'And?' asked Mr Jenkins.

'And what?' said Megan, knowing very well what he wanted to know.

'And, how did you do? Come on, girl, if you're going to go to college, it's important that you do well at school.' Nobody from Mr Jenkins' family had ever gone to college, but now there might be a chance for Megan. He wanted her to get away. The Welsh village of Tredonald where they lived was a coal mining village. Nearly all the men worked down the mine, getting the dirty black coal out of the ground. Mr Jenkins didn't want his daughter to marry a coal miner, or even to spend her life working in the shop – she was too good for that. He hadn't asked Megan what she wanted.

At the other end of the village, Megan's friend, Huw Thomas, was finishing his work for the day.

Huw was also sixteen years old and already tired of life. He worked eight hours a day, five days a week in the village coal mine. There was nothing much else for people in the village. You either worked underground, or you didn't work at all. That was it. But it was better than being a soldier and fighting in some foreign country, like a few of the men in the village. The prime minister in London kept saying the war was nearly over, but Huw wasn't sure if he believed it.

Huw got into the lift at the bottom of the mine with a group of other tired-looking men. Their faces were black from the coal and at first he didn't see his older brother, Gareth, standing opposite him. They smiled at each other, but didn't speak. The lift climbed slowly and noisily up from the dark underground world. Ten dirty faces looked up towards the light.

At the top, it took a few seconds for their eyes to get used to the daylight. They walked over to the bath house, taking in the fresh air. For Huw this was the best moment of the day. He had only been a miner for six weeks, but it felt like longer.

Gareth was waiting for him outside. 'All right, Huw?' asked Gareth. 'How was it today?'

'OK,' Huw said. 'It'll get better, I hope.'

'It will,' his brother replied. 'Look at you. Your arms are stronger already, after only five weeks.'

'*Six* weeks,' said Huw.

Gareth laughed. 'It's hard work, all right. But we're lucky to have jobs. We need the money, with Dad not working.'

Huw couldn't remember the last time his father had had a job. Some days, his father left the house early in the morning and came home with a bit of money, or something for them to eat. And some days he didn't come home at all. Life was not easy for the Thomas family.

The two brothers walked down their street and said 'hello' to the wives, sisters and daughters who had come out of their houses to welcome home their returning men. But outside Huw's house there was no-one to welcome them home. Huw had never known his mother. She had died when he was born. His father and his two brothers, Richard and Gareth, had been his family. And now there was no Richard – killed two years ago while fighting in North Africa.

'Dad!' shouted Gareth. 'We're home. What's for dinner?'

There was no answer.

'Must be out,' said Huw.

'Or in bed,' Gareth said. 'I'll go and look.'

As soon as Gareth entered the bedroom the smell of whisky hit him. His father was asleep on the bed with all his clothes on.

'Drunk again,' Gareth told Huw. 'Where does he get the

money from to go to the pub? You didn't leave any in the house, did you?'

'No, of course not. Except for the money in the box to pay Mr Jenkins for last week's food. But he doesn't know where we keep that, does he?' Huw took out the small box from its hiding place. He opened it. 'He's taken it all!'

'Well,' said Gareth, 'you'll have to go and explain to Mr Jenkins that we can't pay him until the end of the week.' Gareth moved around the small kitchen angrily opening cupboards looking for food. 'And ask him if he'll give us some bread or potatoes. He can add it to next week's bill,' he said.

'Why is it always me who has to explain?' asked Huw.

'Because you're the youngest and Mr Jenkins might feel sorry for you,' replied Gareth. 'Go on, Huw. I'm hungry.'

Huw knew why his father got drunk, but knowing didn't help. He was angry with his father. Nobody would give work to a forty-year-old man with a drink problem, so Huw had had to leave school and start earning money.

Megan looked up from her book and saw Huw coming into the shop. She thought he looked tired and angry.

'Hello, Huw,' she said smiling. 'You OK?'

'Not really . . . the usual things,' said Huw.

Megan and all the village knew about Huw's father. Mr Jenkins listened while Huw explained the latest story. Mr Jenkins felt sorry for Huw, but there was nothing he could do about it. Life was hard for everybody. It was wartime. Other families had lost sons in the war: David Thomas was not the only one. But he was the only one who had started drinking, leaving his two sons to look after themselves.

Megan said, 'Feel like going for a walk later, Huw?' She

and Huw had been friends for years. They used to sit together at school, and out of school they spent a lot of time with each other. Now their friendship seemed to be getting even stronger.

'Yeah, great,' replied Huw. 'I'll come here at about seven. Is that all right, Mr Jenkins?'

'Yes, but not for long, Megan,' said Mr Jenkins, putting a few potatoes in a bag for Huw. 'You've got school tomorrow, remember.'

But Megan knew the real reason that her father didn't want her to be out with Huw for long – he was worried about their continuing friendship. They were not children any more and Mr Jenkins had seen how Huw looked at his daughter.

Chapter 2   *The friendship continues*

Megan lay on the grass by the river with her hands behind her head, looking up at the sky and singing softly.

'Don't move, will you?' said Huw with his back against a tree. 'I'm trying to draw you.'

Megan lay there and enjoyed the warm evening. Sometimes she didn't know what to say to Huw. Since he had started work, their lives were no longer the same, and she knew he was not happy down the mine. But this evening, she felt he was the best person in her life.

'What do you think?' asked Huw as he gave her the drawing. He lay down beside her. 'One day, I'll be rich.'

'Oh yeah, how?' she asked.

'I'll sell my drawings to someone, or maybe I'll go to London and find a good job,' he replied.

'I like your drawings. I think you're a really good artist,' she said. 'But nobody around here has got any money to spend on things like that. And going to London is a bad idea – the war has made it a dangerous place to be.'

'Oh Megan, I can dream, can't I?' replied Huw. 'Don't you have any dreams?'

'Yes, but they seem to change every day,' she said laughing. 'Come on!' Megan jumped up and pulled Huw to his feet. 'Let's walk a bit more, then I'll have to go home.'

'Can I touch your hair, Megan?' asked Huw suddenly. 'It looks so soft.'

Megan was surprised, but she said he could. It was nice to feel his fingers running through her hair. Her face began to burn. Huw looked at her and kissed her. It seemed the right thing to do.

'Don't,' said Megan, but didn't move away. 'If my father could see us now, he'd never let me come out with you again.'

'Sorry,' said Huw, not quite knowing what to do next. There were all sorts of feelings inside him that were new and wonderful. 'Megan, do you like me?' asked Huw, still standing close to her.

'Yes, of course I do,' replied Megan. 'We've been friends for long enough – you know I like you.'

'But I mean ... "like" in a different way, not just as brother and sister,' said Huw. 'I think you're wonderful. Will you be my girl?'

'Oh Huw, yes, I will be your girl,' said Megan. 'But we mustn't tell anyone. My parents ... ' But Huw stopped her.

'And if we both feel the same in two years' time, then I shall ask your father if I can marry you.' Huw's mind was running ahead.

Megan laughed. 'Yes, but for now we must make everyone think that we're still just friends. Nobody must see us holding hands or anything. If my father hears about us, he'll stop me from seeing you. You know what he's like.'

They walked home, happy in each other's company. Huw forgot his problems at home and work, and Megan forgot the college plans her father had for her. She knew he had high hopes for her. And a poor coal miner with a drunken father was not one of them.

Chapter 3   *Romance grows*

Over the next few months, life in the mining village continued in much the same way. When the war in Europe ended, there were wonderful parties in the streets of Tredonald. Everybody hoped that life would be a lot easier – but it wasn't. People worked as hard as ever, and there was still very little to buy in the shops.

Megan and Huw spent as much time as possible together, taking long walks in the evenings or sometimes going to the Saturday night dances in the village.

'Will you dance with me on Saturday, Huw?' Megan asked as they sat together one evening on top of the hill, looking down on the village.

'Of course, if you're not too busy dancing with other men,' he replied.

Huw loved dancing with Megan. It was the one time he could put his arms round her in public. And if they planned it carefully, they were sometimes able to walk home together. They had become good at keeping their love hidden. But they had to dance with other people, too, and Huw hated the way other men held Megan so close that her body was pressed against them.

'What about you?' said Megan. 'You danced with Ruth Hopkins for ages last month . . . and you were laughing!'

Huw remembered that evening, too. He had enjoyed Megan watching him dancing with Ruth. But it had been a quiet walk home that night.

In winter, it became difficult to go for walks. It was dark when Huw finished work and the weather was cold. And every time he went to the shop, Mr Jenkins was there.

'I wish we had somewhere warm to go,' said Megan one cold and windy day in February.

'What are you doing on Saturday evening?' asked Huw.

'Nothing – studying or helping at home. Why?'

'Do you think you could come out?' said Huw. 'There's a new American film on in Afon. Let's go.'

'It's a long way. How will we get there?' Megan asked.

'I'll borrow a couple of bicycles,' said Huw. 'Can you think of something to tell your parents?'

'Not at the moment, but I will before Saturday,' replied Megan. The thought of sitting in a warm, comfortable place with Huw for two hours was wonderful. She would think of some story to tell her parents. Anything.

On Friday afternoon, Huw was on his way home from the mine when he met Gareth on his way to work. The mine was open twenty-four hours a day and Gareth was working nights that week. Huw didn't like it when he and Gareth worked at different times – they never seemed to see each other.

At home, Huw took some money out of the money box. He tried not to think what Gareth would say if he knew. But he wanted to buy Megan a present. This Saturday was going to be a night to remember.

*   *   *

Saturday evening at the cinema was wonderful. Being away from the village made Megan and Huw feel free. For once, they were able to walk down the street holding hands, without thinking about other people seeing them, and in the cinema they both found it difficult to watch the film.

'Huw, stop . . . please,' said Megan quietly after a long kiss. 'We should try and watch a bit of the film.'

But they soon turned to each other again.

The lights went on as the film ended and they stood up slowly. Neither of them wanted to leave. Outside was real life; inside they could be together.

They cycled back towards Tredonald and Megan could feel her heart getting heavier as they got nearer. They stopped just round the corner from her flat.

'This is for you, Megan,' said Huw, giving her a small box. 'I hope you like it.'

He watched her face as she took out the silver necklace.

'It's only second-hand,' he continued. 'One day I'll buy you a new one.'

'Oh Huw, I don't want a new one, this is lovely,' said Megan, putting it round her neck. 'But it must have cost you a lot.' She knew he didn't have much money.

'Come here, my girl,' he said. 'Stop talking and give me a goodnight kiss.'

But suddenly there was a loud noise from the mine.

'Christ!' said Huw. 'What the hell was that!'

But they both knew what it was. It was the sound the village hoped they would never hear. All along the street, doors opened and men and women came out. They ran towards the mine, all thinking of the men who might be caught five-hundred metres below the ground: 'Please God, don't let it be my husband, my brother or my son.'

Chapter 4 *Death at the mine*

People of all ages stood around in small groups, talking in low voices. It was three o'clock in the morning, four hours later. Huw was standing with his father. One look at his father's face had told Huw what he didn't want to know: Gareth was down the mine.

Part of the roof of a tunnel had fallen down and some miners were on the wrong side of the fallen rock. A team of men had been called in to help and had brought up ten men safely. As this group arrived at the top, the waiting families pressed forward looking for their loved ones. Gareth was not one of the ten.

The mine manager came over to Huw and his father. 'There's still hope, David,' he said. 'The team say they can hear noises behind the rock.'

'How many are still down there?' asked Huw.

'Five. It'll take some time before we reach them.'

Huw and his father said nothing, and the mine manager walked away to say the same thing to another family. During the long wait David Thomas and his son, Huw, stood together without speaking. From time to time, one of them lit a cigarette and they drank tea which was given to them by kind neighbours. Megan came and stood with them and put her hand into Huw's. She looked into his eyes and saw he was afraid.

It was ten o'clock when they brought out Gareth's body.

He and two other men had died in the rockfall. The two others had been lucky.

Gareth came home to the small house. His body lay in the front room and his father sat beside him. The neighbours came to say a sad goodbye to the young man they had known so well. Huw's father said nothing as people came and went. He sat by Gareth's side until it grew dark. When Huw came in to say goodnight, it was as if his father hadn't heard.

Huw woke in the middle of the night and couldn't get back to sleep. It seemed wrong to be safe and warm in bed while his brother lay cold downstairs. He decided he would go and sit with Gareth. He got out of bed and walked towards the front room. As he got there, he saw the door was open a little. He stopped. By the light of the moon, Huw could just see his father: he hadn't moved from his son's side. In the quiet, Huw could hear his father's crying and his low voice asking again and again why this had happened. But his words fell into darkness and were lost. Slowly, Huw turned and went back to bed. He stared into the night for a long time and let the hot wet tears run down his cheeks.

For a few days after Gareth's death, Huw's father sat at home. He and Huw slowly began to talk – first about Gareth and then about Richard's death in the war in North Africa. Both of them cried and tried to help each other, but Huw could see that deep inside, his father was angry. Angry because death had taken away three people he loved – his wife, Richard, and now Gareth.

'Just you and me now, boy,' said his father. 'I don't want you to go back down that mine.'

'I've got to, Dad, you know that,' replied Huw. 'What else can I do? There's nothing in Tredonald – only the mine.'

His father said nothing.

That evening Huw met Megan down by the river. It was their first time alone since Gareth's death. She listened as he talked about how empty the house was without his brother. Gareth had taken care of Huw when he was younger and together they had looked after their father. Without him, he felt alone.

'You're not alone,' said Megan. 'You have me. Nothing will change that.' She could see that Huw was hurting inside. She wanted to wash it all away, but knew that the only thing she could do was listen.

Huw loved her for being so strong and understanding. Suddenly, he took hold of both her hands. 'Will you marry me?' said Huw.

'What? Yes, of course I will,' smiled Megan. 'But ... '

'Don't say "but". I know all about the "buts",' replied Huw. 'It's enough that you've said "yes".'

They kissed and only stopped when Megan felt the tears running down Huw's face.

Megan and Huw walked slowly back towards her home.

'Hey look, there's your Mum and Dad,' said Huw, watching as Mr and Mrs Jenkins closed the front door of the shop behind them.

'Yes, they're going to visit Aunt Mary,' replied Megan. 'You can come in, if you like.'

They went upstairs to the flat above the shop where Megan and her family lived. Megan realised it was the first time she and Huw had been there alone. There was a warm fire burning in the sitting room. They sat together on the sofa and talked, and Huw cried some more. Megan held him in her arms until he was quiet. Then they started kissing and their kisses became stronger and stronger.

Megan got up and went out of the room. Huw didn't know what to do, but just then she returned. She had taken off all her clothes and was standing there with the light of the fire behind her.

'Oh Megan, you're beautiful,' said Huw. 'But ... are you sure this is what you want?'

'Yes, Huw,' said Megan in a quiet voice. 'Don't talk, just come to me.'

They made love on the floor. For both of them it was the first time and it was wonderful.

Chapter 5 *Leaving Tredonald*

The day that Huw went back to work, his father started drinking again. It was a terrible day for both of them. Huw had to make himself get into the mine lift. It was very difficult for him to go down to the place where Gareth had died only a week before.

Half an hour after Huw had left the house, David Thomas walked into the Red Lion pub and stayed there all day. His own house was too quiet, and remembering was too painful. Drinking took away all the hurt. So, in the Red Lion, he drank and forgot.

Over the next few weeks, there were days when father and son never met. But one day, Huw got a call from the police station. David Thomas had started a fight in a pub. The police were called and Mr Thomas was taken to the police station.

'He broke some tables and chairs in there, you know,' said the policeman to Huw. 'He's a strong man, your Dad – and even stronger when he's had a bit to drink.'

'I know,' said Huw. 'What happens now?'

'Well, you're lucky,' replied the policeman. 'Old Brian Morgan, the pub manager, said he won't take the matter any further. And we won't either ... this time. But it must never happen again.'

'We can't go on like this,' said Huw to his father, as they walked back home.

'I know, son, I know. I promise I'll stop. It won't happen again, you'll see.'

But David Thomas's promises didn't last very long. Soon he started drinking again. The people in the village had understood at first: 'Poor David, he's had a lot of sadness in his life.' Now it had all changed. Even his friends were no longer so patient with him.

Huw's time with Megan was the only time he felt really happy. Their love for each other was strong. They talked about their present and their future. They talked about Gareth, which was good for Huw. His father often got angry when Gareth's name was spoken at home, but Huw needed to remember his brother.

'You know, Megan,' said Huw very quietly, as they sat on top of the hill. 'My father has got to get away from here. I think it's his only chance of getting his life together. If he stays here, the drink will kill him – one way or another. And I don't think I can let that happen.'

'What are you saying, Huw?' said Megan. She could see from his face that it was difficult for him to speak. And there was a bad feeling growing inside her.

Huw looked at her and continued. 'We had a letter, when Gareth died, from Uncle Edward in Canada. He's Dad's brother. He went to Toronto when I was about four. Anyway, he's asked us to go and live with him. He says he'll send the money for the boat.'

'And do you want to go?' Megan asked.

'Oh Megan, how can you ask that? You know I don't ever want to leave you,' answered Huw. 'But if . . . '

'Can't your Dad go on his own?' Megan's voice was very quiet.

'Don't you see? I'm part of the problem,' said Huw, holding Megan's face in his hands. 'He won't go and leave me working in the mine. I see him looking at me and remembering what happened to Gareth. He hates the mine and everything in Tredonald.'

'And what about us, Huw?' There was sadness in Megan's voice.

'You are the most beautiful thing in my life, Megan,' said Huw. 'I won't lose you. But I have to go with him.' Huw pulled her into his arms and for a few minutes they held each other.

'Do you think you can wait for me?' asked Huw.

'I don't know. What do you mean? Wait until you come back, wait for how long?' Megan began to cry. Huw held her closer.

'Uncle Edward says there's lots of well-paid work in Toronto. It's a big city, not like here. I might even be able to do something with my art. I know I'll be able to earn money quickly, and I won't spend much.' Huw was talking fast now. 'And then, say, in a year I'll be able to pay for you to come out and join me or ... or I'll come back here and we'll get married and both of us can go back to Canada.'

'You seem to have everything planned,' said Megan in surprise.

'No, I haven't, but do you think it's possible?'

'Yes ... oh I don't know ... ' said Megan.

'Shall I talk to your parents about our plans?' asked Huw.

'No, not now,' answered Megan. 'I'll talk to them. I'll have lots of time to choose the right moment.'

'And another thing. If I can earn some good money in

Toronto, your father may realise that I'm different – not just a village coal miner, but someone with a future, someone good enough for his darling daughter.' Huw knew Mr Jenkins would be happy to see him go to Canada.

'Oh, Huw,' said Megan. She couldn't believe how this evening's conversation had completely changed her world.

*   *   *

So on April 28th 1946, David Thomas and his only son, Huw, left the village of Tredonald for a new life in Canada.

For Huw and Megan, saying goodbye was the hardest thing they'd ever had to do. They met in their usual place by the river.

'I'll think about you every day,' Huw said, holding her close and never wanting to let go. 'And I'll write the minute I get there.'

Megan was crying onto his shoulder. 'I know you think I'm a strong person, but when you're in a new country, everything will be different for you. You'll meet a lot of new people. I'll be here doing all the same things. Do you think we'll feel the same about each other in a year's time?'

Huw pulled back and looked deep into her eyes. 'I will, Megan,' he said. 'I know I'll never change.'

They kissed one last time and then she watched as he disappeared. The minute he was gone, Megan felt that a part of her had died.

Part 2   Fifty years later

Chapter 6   *A surprise find*

Tredonald 1996

Megan and her daughter, Beth, sat in the front room of Megan's home. They were going through some old boxes full of cards, old newspapers, photographs and letters.

'Well!' said Beth, looking up from her box. 'I can't believe Grandma and Grandpa kept all these things!'

'I know,' said Megan. Her parents had died some years ago and she had found all these boxes in their bedroom. But until now she had never really looked through them. 'Well,' she continued, 'only one box left.'

'I have to go now, actually,' said Beth looking at her watch. 'Philip's expecting me home by five.' Philip was Beth's husband.

'You go then, dear. I don't want to stop until I've finished everything up here,' Megan said.

'I'll ring you this evening, Mum,' said Beth. 'Don't do too much and make yourself tired.'

'I won't. Thanks for your help earlier,' said Megan. She heard her daughter close the front door.

Megan wanted to finish. She wanted to ring Paul and tell him how well she had done that day. They were getting married in two months and she was moving into his house in London. It was quite a big house, but it was already full of his things. She couldn't take all her parents' things with her as well as her own. She had to throw away a lot.

Megan pulled the last box towards her. She looked inside. More letters. She took out a few and looked at the envelopes. She couldn't believe what she saw. They were all addressed to her and they were all from Canada. And none of them had been opened. She looked at the dates – 1946 and 1947.

'Oh, my God,' she said. 'Huw!'

Her hands were shaking as she started to read one of the letters, dated August 1946.

My lovely Megan

I still haven't received a letter from you. I can't believe it takes four months for letters to cross the Atlantic. What's happened? Is something wrong?

Megan sat for hours reading every letter. At the end she felt completely empty and tired and her heart was full of pain. She remembered all the love that she and Huw had felt for each other when they were young. But more than that, she remembered how terribly hurt she had been when no letters had arrived from him. She had spent many nights crying in her room.

Now she realised what her father had done. He had hidden the letters and watched her unhappiness. She knew that her father had thought Huw was not good enough for her, but she never realised he'd been so much against him.

Megan took the letters downstairs. She sat with them beside her, drank a large whisky and then wrote a letter to Huw. She had no idea if he would ever receive it. 'He won't be at the same address after fifty years – he might even be dead,' she thought to herself. But she knew she had to write.

*   *   *

Toronto 1996

'Dad, letter for you,' shouted Mike Thomas. His father was working in his painting studio at the top of the house.

'OK, Mike, I'll be down in a minute,' said his father, Huw.

Mike put the letter on the kitchen table, and went back into the garden. It was June and the weather was hot, but there was a light wind.

'Where's the letter then?' asked Huw Thomas, standing at the door and holding two cans of beer.

'On the table,' replied his son, taking one of the beers.

Huw picked up the letter and read the postmark 'Tredonald'.

'Wales!' said Huw in surprise. 'Who's writing to me from there? It's years since I had any news from back home.' Huw still talked about Wales as 'home', although he had lived in Toronto all his adult life.

He saw that the letter was addressed to Huw Thomas, 2300 Ontario Drive, Toronto. That was where he and his father had lived in their early years in Toronto. Someone there had discovered where he was living now and had re-addressed the letter.

So who was writing to him? He turned the envelope over in his hands several times. Then he took out the letter and read:

27

Dear Huw

I don't know if this letter will reach you, and I don't really know why I'm writing to you after all these years but . . .

Huw turned to the end of the letter and saw:

With best wishes
Megan

He couldn't believe it. He turned back to the first words of the letter and read:

. . . after all these years but I've just found your letters to me from Canada, when you first got there. Believe me, this was the first time I'd read them and they made me cry, even after fifty years. I found them in a box of my father's papers. They were unopened.

Huw, I never knew that you'd written to me. I thought your new life in Canada had made you forget me. Now I realise that my father kept your letters. I can still remember asking him if there was any post for me and he always said, 'No, he's forgotten you, my girl. I told you he was no good.' Finally, after about a year, I believed him.

But why did he keep the letters? Do you think he wanted me to find them when it was too late? Anyway, he's dead now so I can't ask him. All I can say is I'm sorry. Sorry for what my father did, sorry that you never heard from me, and sorry for . . . everything.

I hope that at least this letter reaches you. Of course, I'll understand if you don't want to write back to me, but if you do, I am still Megan Jenkins and I still live at the same address in Tredonald.

Best wishes
Megan

Huw read the letter again. Megan and their time together in Tredonald came back to him. He had never forgotten her. He couldn't. Every day he looked at her face on the wall of his studio. He had a drawing of her which he'd done when they were sixteen. It had travelled everywhere with him. But to hear from her again . . .

'Are you all right, Dad?' asked Mike, coming into the room.

'I've just heard from someone I knew a long time ago,' Huw replied.

'Is it someone you knew back in Wales?'

'Yeah. I can't believe it really.' Huw explained about Megan and their young love and what he had thought when there were no replies to his letters. He tried to keep his voice light. Mike didn't need to know how deeply they had loved each other.

'Her father sounds terrible,' Mike said when his father had finished.

'Not really. He just wanted the best for his daughter, and he didn't think I was the best,' replied Huw. 'And he never read my letters so he didn't know I was doing well over here.'

'Did Mum know anything about this Megan?' asked Mike carefully.

'I told her that there had been someone else at home, but . . . I mean, I didn't meet your mother until . . . what . . . ten years after I'd left Wales. So Megan was part of my past – part of another life.'

Huw stood up and looked out of the kitchen window across the garden, thinking about Megan – and his ex-wife, Josie. He and Josie were married for twelve years before they got divorced. They said it was because there were too many differences between them, but Huw knew that Megan was part of the problem. Josie always thought he loved Megan more than her. So what he had just said to Mike wasn't really true. Megan had not been only in Huw's past.

Mike came and stood next to him. 'Are you going to write back to her?'

'I don't know,' replied Huw slowly. 'I need time to think about it all. It's all so sudden.'

Huw took the letter and went back upstairs to his studio. He did no painting for the rest of the afternoon. He just sat looking out of the window.

Chapter 7 *Time to decide*

Megan's letter had turned Huw's world upside down. In the days after he received it, he went for long walks by himself. His head was full of things that had happened to him over the last fifty years. He remembered how alone he had felt when no letters had arrived from Megan all those years ago.

At the end of his second year in Toronto, he had had enough money to go back to Wales, but he hadn't gone. He believed that Megan no longer loved him and had forgotten him, so he tried to do the same – forget her.

Both Huw and his father had worked hard in their new country. They had found work in a factory that made cars and David Thomas had stopped drinking. He'd married again and been happy. The Canadian years had been good for his father until he'd died eighteen years ago.

Now Huw was a well-known artist and people paid thousands of dollars for his art. Two months ago, *Time* magazine had even written about him and his latest paintings. His love life, however, had not been so great.

Since his divorce from Josie, there had been other women in his life, but as he got older these friendships seemed less important. His life was full and interesting in other ways – painting, of course, fishing and walking in the forests and mountains. He was happy that Mike and his family were sharing his house. He had more than enough money to do what he wanted. But now Megan had come back into his life.

On one of his many walks, he read Megan's letter for the twentieth time. She said she was still Megan Jenkins. 'So,' Huw thought, 'she never got married.' He remembered her as a warm, loving and intelligent person and thought it was sad that she had never shared all this with a man. Then he laughed at himself. 'Maybe she was happy to be single,' he thought. 'Or maybe she was married and something happened and she changed her name back to Jenkins. What does it matter? It's all in the past now.'

When he arrived back home that evening he told his family that he had made a decision: he was not going to write back to Megan. His life was here now. Better to let the past stay in the past.

Later in the evening, Huw went back upstairs to his studio and, for some reason, started looking through some of his early work. There were paintings and drawings of his that he hadn't looked at for years. He found some drawings he'd done in the first few months after he'd arrived in Toronto. Most of them were of ships. He remembered he used to think about getting on one of the ships and sailing away. Sometimes he had wanted to sail back to Wales and Megan, and then later he'd just wanted to escape to anywhere.

He spent the next few hours lost in his thoughts. It was five o'clock in the morning when he looked at his watch and slowly went to bed, his head still full of the past.

Chapter 8 *Telling Beth*

On Saturday, Megan drove out of Tredonald towards Cardiff. She was on her way to Beth's house for lunch. Her thoughts, however, were not really on the road but on the letters and Huw.

She didn't know if she'd done the right thing writing to Huw. Was it brave or was it just stupid? And what was she going to say to Beth today? And what about Paul? Did she need to tell him about the letters, too? Of course they'd talked about Huw, but it was different now. Huw was no longer safely in the past: he was once again very much part of the present.

But Paul was her present – and her future. At the age of sixty-six, and for the second time in her life, she was making plans to get married. She'd met Paul Henderson some years ago through her work for the Welsh Tourist Office and they'd become good friends. Neither of them were working now so they were able to go on holiday together. Paul had taken her to places like Japan and Peru – places she'd always wanted to visit. And slowly the friendship had developed into something more.

Megan stopped the car outside Beth's house. Beth was in the front garden, waiting for her.

'Morning, Mum,' she said, giving her mother a kiss. 'Journey OK?'

'Yes, fine. It's much quicker now they've opened that

new bit of road, isn't it?' Megan followed her daughter into the house. 'Where's Philip?'

'Playing golf,' replied Beth. 'He'll be back this afternoon.'

Megan was pleased. She loved her son-in-law but what she had to say was for Beth. It would be easier to talk to her alone.

After they'd finished eating, Megan took some of Huw's letters from her handbag and put them on the table.

'I found these the other day,' she said. 'You know, in that last box. After you'd gone home.'

'Who are they from?' asked Beth as she passed her mother a cup of coffee.

'Well, that's just it ...' Megan stopped. She knew that this moment was important for Beth. 'They're from Huw ... Huw Thomas ... your father.'

'My father! Good God!' Beth looked at the envelopes on the table and then looked at her mother. She'd always known about her father – her mother had told her everything when she was young. But for years she'd never thought about him – Huw Thomas was just a name, not a person.

'Here,' said Megan, giving Beth one of the letters. 'You can read this one.'

Beth read it quickly. 'How many more letters are there?' she asked.

'About fifty. They stopped in 1947,' said Megan quietly. 'He didn't write after that.'

'So you never knew anything about them ... That means grandpa or grandma just hid them from you and ... '

'Yes, it was my father, I'm sure. I don't think my mother

34

knew about them either. It was my father who was so against Huw.'

'But you were going to have a baby, you were expecting me. Huw was my father. How could he?' Beth was lost for words.

'I know, Beth. It's difficult to understand. All I can say is my father was doing what he thought was right for me. He wasn't a terrible person.'

'I know,' said Beth. 'I loved him. He was great to me when I was little. That's why it's so hard to believe.'

'My father always wanted me to do well in life,' said Megan, trying to explain. 'He wanted me to go to college and be better than the other young people in the village. He never thought Huw was good enough for me and he clearly thought I would have a better life without him.'

'But that was your decision to make, not his,' said Beth.

'Remember, I was only seventeen – still a child in his eyes. Maybe he was right. I mean, they looked after you when you were a baby and I was able to go to college.' Megan turned to her daughter. 'And we had a good life together, didn't we? We made a happy family.'

'Yes, Mum, it's OK,' said Beth putting her arm round her mother. 'And what about you? How do you feel about it all now?'

'I've written a letter to Huw, but it probably won't reach him. I just felt I had to say something – better late than never.' Megan laughed sadly.

'Did you tell him about me?' Beth asked.

'No, I thought we should wait until … if … he writes back. I hope he does write back. I want to know about his life. Was I wrong not to tell him, do you think?'

'I want him to know about me, if he's still alive,' replied Beth.

'Yes, I understand,' said Megan. 'To tell you the truth, Beth, it's brought back a lot of old feelings. We were very much in love, even though we were so young.'

'I remember you used to talk about him. And he always seemed so wonderful to me as a child.' Neither of the women said anything for a few minutes. Then Beth asked, 'And are you going to tell Paul about all this?'

'Yes, of course. But it doesn't change anything,' said Megan. 'I'm still going to marry Paul.'

Chapter 9 *A second letter*

Huw got another surprise when a second short letter arrived from Wales.

Dear Mr Thomas
I know that my mother, Megan Jenkins, wrote to you two weeks ago. I hope you got that letter. For some reason, I think you did.

'Ah! So she *did* get married,' thought Huw.

She told me about your letters that she'd found, and we talked a lot about you. But there was something in her letter that she didn't say.
It's quite easy for me to write, but probably not easy for you to read. I am your daughter. I was born on November 14th, 1946, seven months after you left Tredonald.
So you can see – if you get this letter – that both of us really would like to hear from you.
With best wishes
Beth Jones

Good God! Was it true? Did he have a daughter? It could be true – the dates were right. He remembered the one and only time that he and Megan had made love. It was quite soon after Gareth's death down the coal mine, and they'd been alone in her parents' flat for the first time.

'I'm sorry, Megan,' said Huw, talking to his drawing of her. 'Did you hate me for what happened?'

He had to write back to Megan. They had a daughter! How strange that sounded! What was she like? There was nothing in Beth's letter to help him get any idea of her. He wanted to meet her, but would she want to meet him? It'd be very difficult for all three of them – there was fifty years of nothing between them.

That night Huw told Mike and Mike's wife, Rebecca, about the letter. Neither of them really knew what to say. Mike found it hard to understand that his father had a daughter, a daughter his father had never known about. To Rebecca it all seemed unreal.

'Wait a minute, Huw,' she said. 'Someone writes to you saying she's your daughter and you believe her? How do you know for sure?'

'It's true,' said Huw slowly. 'In my heart, I know it's true.'

He looked at Mike and Rebecca and said, 'Anyway, I've decided I *am* going to write back to Megan. We'll see what she says.'

Chapter 10 *Writing back*

Two weeks later, it was Megan's turn to receive a letter. When she saw it lying on the floor by the front door, her heart jumped. She knew it was from Huw. She sat with a cup of coffee, looking at the envelope. Finally, she opened it. Some photographs fell out. And there he was – smiling at her. She smiled back at him, her eyes full of tears.

My dearest Megan – after fifty years it's good to say that again. Thank you for writing to me, but why didn't you tell me about Beth? No, I don't think I need to ask that question.

As I'm sure you know, she wrote and explained everything. I think it's wonderful that we have a daughter. But, Megan, I wish . . . so many things!

I'm trying to picture your life with a baby. Did you marry? Did Beth grow up with a father? How much did you hate me all those years for leaving you alone?

I need to know more than letters and photographs can tell me. Would it be all right if I came to Tredonald to see you and Beth? I want the three of us to get to know each other.

I'm sending you some photographs of me and my family. I have a son, Mike, and two lovely grandchildren . . .

Megan read to the end of the letter. Beth had told her about writing to Huw, so that wasn't a surprise. But to actually read his words and see his face again – it was almost too much for her.

It was time for Megan to speak to Beth. They had to make a decision together. Did they want Huw back in their lives, or should they continue as before – just the two of them. And then there was Paul to consider.

Huw waited impatiently for an answer from Megan. In his head, he had many wonderful conversations with the two of them. But he knew that it was not going to be that easy.

Then soon after his letter to Megan, he received a reply – just a short letter with a photograph of two women.

'My God!' he said quietly, talking to her photo. 'Just look at you! You're still my lovely Megan. And this is our daughter, is it? Yes it is, I can see it is.'

He then turned to the letter and read it through until he reached the final two lines:

PS Here's a photo of Beth and me which was taken in the sitting room above the shop. Remember?

Remember? How could he forget – they had loved each other in that same room fifty years before. He remembered the feel of her soft lips and the smell of her dark hair.

He looked back at the photograph. The two women were sitting on a sofa together and holding hands, both of them looking at the camera and smiling. Huw stood in front of the studio window and cried. So many years had passed and so much time lost. Seeing how close Megan and her daughter were, it was painful to think that he had not been a part of it. He turned the photograph over. On the back was the date and the words, 'Beth and I would like to meet you.'

Chapter 11   *Home to Wales*

Huw, Mike and Rebecca were sitting in the garden of their house, drinking wine on a warm evening.

'So that's my half-sister, is it?' asked Mike, looking closely at the photo.

'Let's see,' said Rebecca. 'Oh yes! Look at her nose, Mike. It's just like yours!'

'Rubbish!' said Mike. He turned the photo over and read the message. 'Are you going over to see them, Dad?'

'Yes, I think so. Is that OK with you?'

'It's a big step, but how can you not go and see your daughter?' replied Mike. 'You'd never be able to live with yourself.'

'And Megan, too,' said Huw. 'I do want to see her again.'

'Hey, how about this for an idea?' said Mike suddenly. 'I'll come with you. I'd be really interested to see Tredonald. It's part of our family's life, isn't it? You and grandpa never really talked much about the place. You just used to say that Toronto was much better.'

'Yes, I know,' said Huw with a laugh. 'We arrived just after the war in Europe. Life was very difficult in Wales when we left.'

'How about it then? You and me,' said Mike. He was getting quite interested in the idea of travelling with his father.

'Another time, Mike,' said Huw quietly. 'This time is for me. OK?'

'OK,' said Mike, and then added, 'as long as you don't decide to stay in Wales.'

'Don't worry,' said Huw. 'I'm not going to stay there. My home is in Canada, my work is here, you're here. I'll be back.'

*   *   *

So at the end of the month, Huw flew to London. He'd written to Megan, and to Beth, to say that he was coming, but hadn't said which day. He'd decided not to, then he could change his mind at the last minute if he wanted to. But now the plane was about to land.

His hire car was waiting for him outside the airport. He had slept well on the plane so he was able to keep a clear head for driving. And he needed it – driving on the left was not easy!

The nearer he got to Tredonald, the more unsure he became. He realised that he was afraid of what might happen. Half of him was afraid that he wouldn't like Megan, or Beth, and the other half of him was afraid he would like them too much. He was a man who liked to know what he was doing and why. Before he'd received Megan's first letter, his life had been well organised, but now it was different – he felt like a sixteen-year-old again.

It was not just Megan and Beth – it was also Tredonald. He and his father had left it so long ago and at a really bad time in their lives. He had no idea how he was going to feel when he saw the place again.

Just outside Tredonald, he stopped at a pub. He needed a drink.

The barman put a glass in front of him. 'Are you here on holiday?' he asked.

'Sort of,' replied Huw.

'We don't get many people here on holiday. There's nothing to do here, nothing to see really.'

'I used to live here many years ago,' said Huw.

'Did you now?' The barman looked a bit more interested. 'You'll see some changes then.'

'Mmm,' said Huw, trying to enjoy his rather warm beer. 'What about the mine in Tredonald? Is it still working?'

'No, it closed about fifteen years ago. Well, it's still open but only for tourists, not for coal.'

But Huw didn't want to talk any more. 'Is there a public phone I can use?' he asked.

'Through there,' said the barman showing him a door to the left of the bar.

Huw went through it. He picked up the phone and rang Megan's number.

Chapter 12 *A new start*

'Oh damn!' said Megan. 'Why does the phone always ring when I've just sat down? Hello?'

'Hello, this is Huw. Is that Megan?'

'Huw! Where are you? You sound so close!' Megan began to shake.

'I'm in the Rose and Crown, just outside Tredonald,' said Huw.

'Oh, Huw, why didn't you … ' And then she couldn't continue.

Neither of them spoke for a few seconds. Neither could quite believe they were so close to the person they'd lost fifty years ago. When Megan finally said something, her voice was full of tears. 'Let's meet in the Tredonald Arms Hotel. It's on Bridge Street. Do you remember it?'

'No, but I'll find it. See you there in half an hour?'

'No, I need a bit more time,' said Megan. She wanted some time to get herself and her thoughts together. 'Let's meet a bit later … say seven o'clock?'

'Fine,' replied Huw. 'And Megan … it's good to hear your voice. I can't really believe I'm talking to you again.' From the moment Megan had answered the phone, Huw had felt sure again. He wasn't worried about how the meeting would be – he was just impatient to see her.

'I know, Huw,' said Megan quietly. 'I'm happy you're here.'

As soon as she finished talking to Huw, Megan rang

Beth. 'He's arrived,' she said, knowing she didn't need to say who had arrived.

'And? Have you seen him?' asked Beth. Megan didn't reply immediately. 'Are you all right, Mum?'

'Yes, sorry dear, I'm meeting him at seven. But I don't feel very brave. I think I'm sorry I wrote to him. I mean . . . what are we going to talk about? Oh Beth, it's all too much for me!'

'Don't worry, Mum,' said Beth. 'I'm sure it'll be fine. Just take it as it comes. Ring me later. And remember, I love you.'

At seven o'clock that evening, Megan walked into the Tredonald Arms Hotel. Huw was sitting in a big armchair, opposite the front entrance where he could watch everybody who came in. They saw each other immediately.

What he saw was a slim woman with grey hair and a strong face. What she saw was a tall, handsome man whose face was brown from the sun. They shook hands, and then he kissed her on both cheeks. They both stood looking at each other for a few moments without saying anything. Then Megan sat down in the soft armchair.

For the next two hours, they talked. At first, the conversation had been a bit difficult with lots of 'I can't believe it!' and 'Is it really you?' and 'After all these years'. But slowly they began to talk as old friends. It was easy to talk about their homes, work, Tredonald and Toronto. But it was more difficult to find the right words when they talked about Beth.

'Megan, tell me about Beth, our daughter. I want to know everything,' said Huw.

'I don't think of her as *our* daughter, I'm afraid,' replied

Megan carefully. 'I've been her only parent all her life. Of course I've talked to her about you, but you've never been a real person for her.'

'I'm sorry,' said Huw quickly. 'I didn't mean to ... You're right, of course. But I want to know all about her.'

'Well,' replied Megan in a more friendly voice. 'She lives in Cardiff, she's married with three grown-up children, so you have three grandchildren as well.'

'That makes five. My son Mike has two – David and Amy.'

Megan nodded and continued. 'She and her husband have their own business – they're architects. Beth was always interested in drawing ... '

'Like me,' said Huw, pleased that he shared something with his daughter. Then he became more serious. 'Your father really hated me, didn't he? He preferred to let you be an unmarried mother rather than marry me.' Huw felt himself getting angry.

'I don't think he hated you – it was more that he really loved me, or maybe his ideas for me,' replied Megan.

'Was it hard for you when she was born?'

'Yes and no,' replied Megan, sitting back in her chair. 'When I told my parents I was pregnant, they were angry ... sad, hurt ... everything. My father had big plans for me – do you remember? After I had Beth, I went to college and became a teacher, and he and my mother looked after Beth. They were wonderful, really. They loved her and she had a happy time as a child. It was only when she used to ask about her daddy that the conversation went cold. But she soon learnt. Her daddy was somebody she asked *me* about, not her grandparents.'

A little bit of sadness had come into Megan's voice. Huw took her hand and, for a few seconds, she didn't realise. Then she gave a smile and took her hand away. 'Anyway, now it's your turn. I want to know more about you. You've done very well with your art, haven't you? I'm so pleased.'

She was able to look at him as he talked about his work and she could see the same Huw that she'd known all those years ago. She wanted to reach across and touch him, to reach across fifty years . . . But how could she?

It was a fine evening so they went for a short walk. Huw needed some fresh air. He felt tired after his long journey from Toronto, but he didn't want to say goodnight to Megan. They stood looking down at the river.

'We used to spend a lot of time walking by this river, didn't we?' said Huw. 'Do you remember?'

'Yes, we did,' laughed Megan. 'Well, we didn't have many places. It was either here or up on the hill, wasn't it?'

'True,' said Huw. 'And the cinema. We went there the night Gareth was killed.'

'Yes, I remember it well,' replied Megan. 'I often think of Gareth.'

'Really? Why's that?' asked Huw, surprised.

'I sometimes take groups of visitors on tours down the mine,' replied Megan. 'The tour takes people past the entrance to the tunnel where the roof fell. Gareth is always in my thoughts when we pass it.'

Huw turned towards her. 'But why are you – I mean, when did you start going down the mine?'

'Oh, it's a long story,' said Megan. 'But when we knew that the mine was going to close, I had the idea of trying to do something with it. I'd stopped teaching so I had the time. I don't go down very often now. Most of the tours are done by the older ex-miners. That was another reason for not letting it die. There was nothing else for the men to do. Now at least some of them have jobs.'

'Good for you,' said Huw. 'You always were a fighter, weren't you? I think I'd like to go down again. Would you come with me?'

'You don't need me. You know it better than I do,' said Megan.

'I did, but not now. Come with me.'

'OK,' said Megan. 'If you really want to.'

As they walked back towards the hotel, Megan told him more about her work for the mine. She explained how difficult it had been to get money to develop the mine so they could open it to tourists.

'It took five years, and it was hard work – but I met some interesting people, including a very dear person, Paul Henderson, who ... helped me a lot.' Megan had meant to say 'who I'm going to marry next month', but she didn't. At least she'd introduced Paul's name into the conversation: now she could talk about him, and maybe the next time she met Huw she would tell him she was going to get married.

Chapter 13   *Lunch with Beth*

Huw was working down the mine. Suddenly there was a loud noise and the roof of the tunnel began to fall. He put his arms over his head, but the falling rock knocked him to the ground. He could see Megan's hands reaching out to him, but he couldn't quite touch them. Then more rock fell and all was black. He cried out and woke up. He sat up in bed and for a moment couldn't remember where he was. He looked around and slowly realised that this was his hotel room in Tredonald. He was safe, not down the mine. He lay down again, but couldn't go back to sleep.

It was five o'clock in the morning. He got up and sat by the window of his room watching the darkness disappear and the sun rise. His head was full of thoughts – Megan, Gareth, his father, Beth – and how life threw things at you when you were least expecting them. One thing was clear to him, however, and that was how he felt about Megan. He loved her. Maybe not in the same way as he had when he was seventeen, but he knew that she was still the only one for him. Being with her again felt right – it was like coming home. He wanted to be with her for the rest of his life. He was sure about this. And Megan? What did she feel about him? In the next few days, he would find out.

He got back into bed and fell into a deep sleep. It was the sound of the telephone that woke him.

'Mr Thomas,' said a voice. 'There's a lady here in reception for you.'

'Thank you,' said Huw, looking at the clock. 'Tell her I'll be down soon.'

It was ten o'clock! Megan was waiting for him. They were going to Cardiff to meet Beth. He had the fastest shower ever, got dressed and was downstairs in the hotel reception in fifteen minutes.

'Sorry, Megan,' he said, giving her a kiss on the cheek. 'I had a bad night. I was still asleep when the phone rang.'

Megan smiled. 'Would you like me to drive? You can take it easy.'

'Good idea,' replied Huw, returning her smile. He was happy to see her and to know that they were going to spend the day together.

As Huw opened the door of the car for Megan, he saw that she was wearing a silver necklace. 'Megan, you've still got it!'

'What?' said Megan, but her hand immediately moved to touch the necklace. 'Oh, the necklace. Yes, of course I've still got it. I often wear it.'

Huw sat beside her as they drove out of Tredonald. She told him how important the necklace had been to her in the early days. It was the only thing she had from him – except for Beth, of course. Huw told her about the drawing he had of her and how it went everywhere with him.

Megan felt comfortable with Huw next to her. She, too, had not had a very good night's sleep – too many things going round in her head. But today she felt better. She started talking about Beth. She knew that Beth was a bit worried about meeting her father for the first time, and she thought that Huw was probably feeling the same.

Megan and Huw entered the café where they were

meeting Beth. Huw's eyes searched left and right, looking for the right face. A tall woman with dark hair stood up and walked towards them. She put her arms round Megan and held her for a moment. Then she looked at Huw, put out her hand and said, 'Hello, I'm Beth.'

'Hello, I'm ... ' Huw stopped himself from saying 'I'm your father' and said, 'I'm Huw.' He took both her hands in his. They looked long and hard at each other, searching for something that showed they were father and daughter.

Megan spoke. 'Look, I'm going to do some shopping. I think it's better if you two talk without me here. I'll be back in about an hour or so.' And without giving either of them time to say anything, she walked out of the café.

From the moment Huw and Beth sat down, they didn't stop talking. She told him about growing up in the flat above the shop in Tredonald, about her life now, her kids, her husband. She was completely comfortable with him.

'Mum loved you, you know,' said Beth. 'Even when she didn't hear from you, she still loved you. In fifty years, she didn't say one bad thing about you. Not like grandpa – he didn't like hearing your name.' Beth laughed.

'I loved her, too,' said Huw. 'The first years in Canada were so difficult for me without her.'

'She's a wonderful person,' said Beth warmly. 'I hope she's going to be happy now.'

'I want to make her happy,' replied Huw, not understanding Beth's words. 'Beth, I still love her. I want to marry her.'

'Oh!' said Beth, and realised her mother had not told Huw about Paul. She had to say something.

'Huw, has she talked to you about Paul, Paul Henderson?' asked Beth.

'She said he was a friend – why?' Beth was quiet and Huw added, 'Is there something more between them?'

'Yes,' said Beth. 'They're planning to get married next month. Mum's going to move to London.'

'Does she love him?' asked Huw, quietly.

'I think so ... I don't know really ... You'll have to ask her.' Beth liked Paul very much and believed that he was good for her mother. She thought they would have a happy future together. But she also knew that things were no longer that easy now Huw had come back into their lives. She knew her mother still felt very deeply about Huw – but it wasn't for her to say anything. Her mother must decide for herself.

'Have you told her how you feel?' asked Beth.

'No, it's too soon. I want to give her time to love me again. Then I will. I'm not going to lose her a second time,' said Huw quietly.

'I'm sure Mum will tell you about Paul. She doesn't like hiding things. And anyway, he's coming to Tredonald at the weekend. We're all having dinner together. Maybe you can meet him and see what you think.' Beth looked at Huw carefully and added, 'Please be careful. I love my mother very much. I don't want anybody to hurt her.'

Huw touched Beth's hand and said, 'I won't hurt her – not again.'

Beth smiled at him and then looked up to see her mother coming into the café.

Chapter 14 *In love*

On the drive back to Tredonald, Huw talked about Beth – how much he liked her, what a warm person she was, how he wanted to see more of her. He'd decided it was safer to talk about Beth rather than about him and Megan.

'She's coming up to Tredonald on Saturday, to have dinner with you and Paul, isn't she? Perhaps I'll be able to spend a little more time with her then,' said Huw.

'Yes, that's a good idea,' said Megan. 'Beth's told you about Paul – that we're getting married? Yes, of course, she did. I'm sorry, Huw, I did mean to tell you yesterday, but it didn't seem the right time.'

'When are you marrying him?' asked Huw.

'21st September. I'm in the middle of selling the shop and the flat at the moment. And when that's all finished, I'll move to London.' Megan didn't feel very comfortable talking to Huw about her future life with Paul. However, he seemed to be OK about it.

'And what about Tredonald and all your friends here? And Beth in Cardiff? Won't you miss it all?' asked Huw.

'Yes, of course,' said Megan quietly. 'It'll be strange at first, but I'm ready for a change. The mine is working well – they don't need me anymore. Beth and the grandchildren have their own lives. And Paul and I haven't hurried – we've got to know each other very well – and I know we'll be happy together. I've told him about you, and I'd like you to meet him on Saturday. Will you join us for dinner?'

'Thank you, I'd like to. And can I ask you, Megan ... do you love him?' Huw had to ask. He couldn't just continue being nice. He couldn't hide what he felt any longer. 'Do you feel that you can't live without him? Are you happy every time you see him or hear his voice on the phone? Can you ...?' Huw had many more questions that he wanted Megan to answer, but she stopped him.

'Huw! Why are you asking me all this?' asked Megan, in surprise. 'It isn't any of your business how I feel about Paul!'

'Maybe not,' replied Huw. 'But I want you to be sure that you're doing the right thing, and for the right reasons.'

Megan stopped the car at the side of the road and turned to face Huw. 'Of course I'm sure,' replied Megan a little angrily.

'Because I think we still love each other,' said Huw. 'Well, perhaps I should say that I *know* I love you. I've always loved you. Even when I was married to Josie, deep inside I knew that – and I think she did too. And I think you still feel something for me, don't you?'

Megan sat looking straight ahead. She didn't know what to say.

'I don't want you to marry Paul,' he continued. 'I want you to marry me. And I've got about two weeks to make you feel that, too.' Huw hadn't meant to say it quite like that, but he wanted Megan to be clear about how he felt – and he didn't have very much time.

'Huw, you can't just come back into my life after fifty years and start organising everything. You don't love me, how can you? You don't know me. I think it's wonderful that we've been able to meet again and become friends. But my future is with Paul.'

'Megan, I won't say any more about it. But I just want you to promise that you'll think about what I've said,' Huw said quietly.

'How can I forget it?' thought Megan to herself.

Megan started the car and they drove back to Tredonald without saying a word to each other. Huw got out at his hotel and they said goodbye. He said he would phone her the next day, but they made no other plans. Huw felt it was better to give Megan some time alone – even though he wanted to be with her every minute of every day.

Chapter 15 *An old photograph*

Huw was right. Megan did need time alone. Here she was, a woman of sixty-six, and two men wanted to marry her! Of course she was not going to marry Huw. He didn't really love her. He'd just flown half way around the world, and in two days had met his old love and a daughter he never knew he had. It was not surprising that he was saying things he didn't really mean.

The next morning, Megan did some more packing. But it was difficult for her to escape from thoughts of Huw. Everything that she put into boxes or cases seemed to throw her back to some time in the past. And the past was Huw.

She rang Paul to check what time he was arriving the next day. He asked her how things had gone between Huw and Beth and she told him it had gone well. They talked for a while about other things and then Megan told him that Huw was joining them for dinner. Paul said that was fine. She didn't know if that was how he really felt. But it was nice and easy talking with him, and she felt safe.

After she'd put the phone down, she remembered what Huw had asked her: 'Are you happy every time you hear his voice?' What kind of question was that? It was the sort of thing you felt when you were in love for the first time, not when you were her age.

Then the phone rang again and this time it was Huw. He told her he'd been walking round the village and had met someone that they'd been 'at school with, and how they'd had a laugh about the old days. Then he said that he'd like to meet her for a drink and maybe dinner if she would like to.

'Seven o'clock at your hotel?' asked Megan. 'It'll be good to escape from the flat tonight.'

'Wonderful. See you then,' said Huw.

The conversation had been light, friendly and ... and Megan had been very happy to hear his voice.

Just after seven that evening, Megan joined Huw in the dining room of his hotel. Huw could see that she was a little tired so he didn't talk about the two of them. He told her about the wonderful wild areas in the north of the country, and funny stories about the art world in Canada and how much he loved living there. Two hours passed in easy happy conversation.

'Now, you tell me something,' said Huw, smiling at her.

'Well, you know you said you saw Brian Perkins earlier today,' said Megan. 'I found this – look.'

And she passed Huw a black and white photograph. He looked closely at it and saw a group of about thirty children aged thirteen or fourteen, all standing very straight and smiling at the camera. It was an old school photograph.

'And look, there's you at the back with Brian Perkins,' Megan laughed. 'And there's me, just below you. We all look so young and fresh, don't we?'

'And I'm the only one not looking at the camera. I'm looking at you! You see, even then I was only interested in you,' said Huw.

Megan moved on. She didn't want to give Huw the chance to talk about her. She had brought some other photos for him to look at – photos of friends and her family, and photos of Beth when she was a baby. She gave the ones of Beth to Huw, saying, 'Would you like to keep these?'

Huw put them in his pocket.

'Time for me to go, I think,' said Megan.

'I'll walk home with you,' said Huw. They walked to her home through the quiet streets of the village.

'I'm happy I came back to see Tredonald,' said Huw. 'It's not the terrible place I remember. I'm sure I can put the past behind me now.'

'Good,' said Megan – and then thought, 'Does that mean me as well?'

But at her front door Huw said, 'Megan, I can feel that all evening you've been hoping that I won't say anything about us. And I won't, except I meant what I said yesterday.'

'Please Huw, let's not talk about it,' said Megan. 'Tomorrow you're going to meet Paul – the man I'm going to marry.' Megan took hold of his hands. 'Thank you for a lovely evening. I'll see you here tomorrow.'

Megan went to bed that night knowing that tomorrow's dinner was going to be difficult for all of them.

Chapter 16   *Dinner for five*

'Paul, this is Huw. Huw, Paul.' Megan introduced the two men who shook hands. Then she disappeared into the kitchen and left them to make conversation. Beth and Philip were late. She wanted them here now – she needed help.

'I don't know what's happened to Beth and Philip,' she said, walking over to the window of the sitting room. Huw and Paul seemed to be talking quite happily.

'Probably Philip was late finishing his game of golf,' said Paul, going over to stand by Megan's side. 'He lives for his golf at the weekends, doesn't he? Do you want another drink, love?'

'No, I'd better not. Oh, here they are now. Good.' And Megan once again disappeared out of the room.

'Sorry we're late, Mum. My fault,' said Beth.

'That's OK,' she said. Beth and Philip both gave her a kiss. 'I'll just go and finish off in the kitchen. Dinner will be about ten minutes.'

From the kitchen she could hear Paul laughing, and then Beth. 'Oh good,' she thought. 'Maybe it's all going to be fine. Maybe I don't need to worry at all.'

At dinner the conversation went well. Beth and Philip wanted to know all about Huw's art, and Huw enjoyed talking about it. Paul also joined in – he knew an artist in London who had bought one of Huw's paintings. Megan was able to sit back and listen; Paul looked over at her and smiled.

Megan watched, listened, joined in the conversation – and compared. It was a terrible thing to do, but she found that she was comparing Paul and Huw. Huw with his brown face, his stories and the past that they shared. And kind Paul who'd made her feel good again, and who was her future. It was strange to see the two halves of her life here in the same room.

Once or twice she saw Huw looking a little sad – when Beth had said something about her younger life. And she realised that he was trying hard to keep the conversation light, and not ask too many questions about the past.

At midnight, Huw stood up to go. The others were staying the night at Megan's. 'Don't forget, Megan, we're meeting at ten tomorrow morning for our tour of the mine.'

'I haven't forgotten. I'll leave everybody here doing the washing-up and I'll see you at the entrance to the mine.'

Everybody stood up to say their goodbyes. Paul shook his hand and said, 'I've enjoyed meeting you, Huw, and maybe some day Megan and I can visit you in Canada. I'd love to try that fishing you were telling me about.'

Huw said nothing but just smiled. At the door, he turned and said, 'Paul, I believe that you're a good man and I hope you and Megan will be very happy together.' He kissed Beth and Megan. As the door closed behind him, Beth looked at her mother.

Chapter 17 *Time to go*

At ten the next morning, Huw and Megan stepped into the lift to go down the mine. It was a modern lift – not like the one that Huw remembered. He felt as if he was in a large shop rather than a coal mine. But when the doors opened at the bottom, he was immediately taken back fifty years. It was the smell. You might be able to make everything modern, but you could never lose the smell of coal, he thought. He followed Megan down one of the tunnels. It was lit now, but he didn't need the light. He knew that he'd be able to find his way around with his eyes closed.

It was a quiet world down there. The last miner had left years ago.

'Do you mind if I walk a bit by myself?' Huw asked Megan. He wanted to have some private time to remember Gareth.

'Of course,' said Megan. 'I'll wait here.'

She watched him walk away from her with his hands in his pockets. This morning she felt flat – maybe even a bit sad. The feeling had come to her last night, when Huw had wished her and Paul a happy life together. She realised that Huw had accepted her and Paul as a couple. So he didn't want to marry her after all, he didn't love her – why did that make her feel sad? She should be pleased that he was not going to make things difficult for her.

Huw came back. 'What a short life poor Gareth had,' he said quietly.

'I know,' said Megan, and she reached out to take his hand.

'The night he died was just … ' Huw didn't continue, but Megan knew what he felt – she remembered that terrible night too.

They walked towards the lift hand in hand. 'You OK?' asked Megan quietly.

'Yes and no.' Huw looked down at her and said, 'I've decided to go back to Toronto. I'm flying tomorrow evening.'

'Oh Huw, why so soon?' Megan was completely shaken.

'It's no good, Megan. I realise that I can't just arrive after fifty years, tell you I love you and expect you to leave everything and come away with me. So I've decided to go back early. There's no reason for me to stay any longer.'

'But what about Beth?' asked Megan. 'Don't you want to spend some more time with her?'

'Yes, and I will, but not now,' answered Huw. 'I'll write to her, of course, and I hope I'll be able to see her again either here or in Canada.'

'So, you're going away again, and leaving us,' said Megan. 'Beth is going to be very sorry.'

'I don't feel there's anything else I can do, Megan. I've told you how I feel – I love you and I want to marry you. It would hurt too much to watch you and Paul together, or to hear you talking about him.'

They reached the top of the mine and walked out into the sunshine.

'Oh Huw, I don't know what to say,' said Megan. 'I don't want you to go, I feel as if I'm just getting to know you again. Everything has happened so quickly in the last few days – but they've been wonderful days.'

Outside Megan's home, Huw turned and took her hands.

'I'm leaving Tredonald after breakfast tomorrow, so I think this is goodbye – for now,' Huw found it difficult to speak. 'I'll keep in touch with you and Beth, of course. I'm not sorry I came back, but I wish with all my heart that the ending could be different. Goodbye, sweet Megan. Be happy.'

Huw kissed her lips, her eyes, her nose – everywhere on her face. Then he walked away. He turned around once and saw that Megan was still standing outside her front door. He gave a little wave. His face was wet with tears.

*   *   *

The next morning, Huw packed his suitcase, feeling bad. He stopped when he came to the photo of Megan and Beth, and looked at it with love. He remembered how fifty years ago, when he was about to leave for Canada, he had packed his drawing of Megan with the same feeling of love. Then, there had been all those years without her. Finding her again had been so wonderful, but now the future seemed empty.

Downstairs, Hugh paid his hotel bill at reception and walked out to his car. As he was getting in, he heard someone behind him and turned round. There was Megan. They looked at each other for a few seconds and then fell into each other's arms.

'Oh, Huw, I've been awake all night thinking about you. I kept remembering how I felt when you left me fifty years ago. I can't let you leave me again. You're part of me – I feel complete with you.'

'What do you want me to do then?' asked Huw softly, loving the sound of Megan's words.

'Ask me to marry you again,' she replied in a shaking voice.

'Megan, marry me. Be my girl again,' Huw said.

'Of course, Huw,' she answered. 'Of course.'

They were both crying. They cried because of the years they had lost – years they would never get back. But they also cried because they were happy. They still had time: they had tomorrow and the next day and the next ... They had a second chance of a wonderful future together and this time nothing would go wrong.